# DIGITAL MARKETING MADE EASY

Copyright © 2019 Catherine Skeet-Yaffe

The right of Catherine Skeet-Yaffe to be identified as the author of this work has been asserted in accordance with the copyright, Designs and Patens Act 1988

ISBN: 9781796713336

All rights reserved. This book or any portion thereof may not be reproduced or used in any manner whatsoever without the express written permission of the author except for the use of brief quotations in a book review.

# Contents

Introduction ........................................................................................ 1
How to use this book ......................................................................... 5
Glossary .............................................................................................. 7
Chapter One - Planning your journey ................................................ 9
Chapter Two - Finding Your Market ................................................ 21
Chapter Three - Building Know, Like and Trust .............................. 36
Chapter Four - List Building Made Easy .......................................... 42
Chapter Five - Sales Funnels ............................................................ 55
Chapter Six - Email Marketing ......................................................... 70
Chapter Seven - Email Nurturing ..................................................... 79
Chapter Eight - Your 28 Day Digital Road Map ............................... 85
Final Words ....................................................................................... 90
Acknowledgements .......................................................................... 92
About the author .............................................................................. 93

# Introduction

*"I had what I thought was a brilliant idea for a business - how to get free PR. Based on my years as a freelance journalist and business magazine editor I knew that editors and journalists were screaming out for content, so I went about setting up a business that would teach other businesses how to get free publicity. I assumed everyone would snap my hand off, be willing to pay for 1:1 support and I'd be raking it in - I couldn't have been more wrong! The market had moved on, I didn't understand my target market and had no clue what people were looking for. It lasted 6 months."*

This was me a few years ago. I have made so many mistakes, not just with that business idea but with others too.

I've been involved with the world of Digital Marketing since 2008, from starting an agency in my back bedroom to having a team of seven, a business partner and swanky offices.

I've owned (and sold) a magazine in pursuit of my childhood dream of being a journalist.

I've worked for other people, generated millions of pounds worth of sales and still ended up being made redundant.

In 2018 everything I had learned and failed at, all my experience - business and otherwise -  came together with the creation of Herding Cats Digital, Digital Marketing Made Easy.

I knew there had to be an easier way to start a business and use the internet to grow it. I had done exactly that when we owned the digital agency, Cat Creative Media, and as I looked around the internet I couldn't understand why more businesses weren't making use of the tools available to them to grow a sustainable business.

I realised that whether you're an emerging entrepreneur or if you've been in business for a while, navigating the internet and building a business is overcomplicated, overwhelming, intimidating and downright confusing.

There's so much STUFF out there! And LOTS of snake oil advice - even as an experienced online marketer I still found myself falling for every 6-figure launch model out there.

So, I made a commitment to MAKE IT EASY.

Easy for you as an emerging entrepreneur.
Easy for you if you're an established business owner.
Easy to take advantage of the tools available to you, easy to follow a digital roadmap, easy to put all the building blocks in place to enable you to build and grow your business online - easily and effortlessly.

Well, not quite effortlessly (there is work involved!) but it really doesn't have to be complicated.

## Who is this book for?

I'd like to think that if you've picked up this book then you're looking for an easier way.

You know that using the internet is the best way to grow your business. Whether you have a smoking hot new idea, or you've been in business for a while, you know that you're not taking advantage of the online world with your marketing.

You may have tried several ideas already and seen no return (social media anyone?).

Perhaps you've heard of a lead magnet, a landing page and a digital sales funnel but it's left you bamboozled.

Maybe you too have fallen for the snake oil sales pages and downloaded every freebie out there only to be left more confused than you were before.

You could have fallen down the YouTube wormhole, only to be found 3 hours later in tears of frustration and no further forward.

We've all done it, it's an easy trap to fall into, and IT ENDS NOW. Right here with this book. I've got you, my friend, together we can do this - I promise.

## My promise to you

I promise that by the time you have finished with this book you will have a very clear roadmap for starting your digital marketing strategy.

Terminology will be kept to a minimum and where it is used there will be an explanation. I've also included a glossary that you can refer back to at any time.

There will be no overwhelm, and the advice I share is based on my own experiences with my business and also that of the businesses I have worked with. No fluff, no hype, no BS.

I PROMISE

# How to use this book

The book is broken into chapters, and then into sections to make it easy for you to follow.

Within each section, there are lists of Action Steps for you to take as you start implementing the steps you need.

Each section is clearly explained and at the end of each section, there is a summary highlighting the action points.

The book also contains online resources that are only available to you, and are complementary to you, the reader. You will see these marked as URL's, so you can easily access them.

Feel free to read the book through then go back to the beginning and complete each chapter as and when you feel ready.

Keep it on your desk so that you have a handy reference to refer back to when you get stuck or feel yourself stalling. But most importantly, enjoy the process.

## What you will know by the end of the book

This book delves deeper into the Why than other similar books that are on the market, and there's a very good reason for this.

Quite often How-To books list a set of instructions without being 100% clear on the outcome you can expect, or why you're expected to do it that way.

Although there are How To resources dotted throughout this book, from my experience it's even more important to understand the Why of something.

Why is it important to conduct research?
Why do you need to spy on your competitors?
Why do you need to build know, like, trust?

Once you understand the fundamentals, everything else will fall into place and make perfect sense. You'll understand WHY you're doing something and how it all fits in with the bigger picture of your business, and how you're going to grow it.

By the end of this book will you have an overview of everything you need to have in place to build your very own digital roadmap, one that is unique to you and your business, one that works, and one that won't leave you feeling overwhelmed, exhausted or confused.

You will have clarity, focus and all the tools you need to grow a wildly successful business whilst living your ideal life.

# Glossary

Throughout the book I use terms that relate to various processes and tools that you will come across throughout out your digital journey. I've listed them here with a brief explanation for ease.

**Target Audience or Target Market** - the wide group of people you want to work with
**Ideal Client / customer** - the individual prospect you would like to work with
**Niche or Niching Down** - Narrowing the selection of your target market
**Long Form Post** - A social media update that is above 100 words
**Social Proof** - Public acknowledgement of how amazing you are to work with
**Case Studies** - A short description of a customer you have worked with and the outcome
**Call To Action** - An instruction or direction that you want people to take
**Upsell** - An opportunity to sell an advance or upgrade on an original purchase
**Header** - The area at the top of your website
**URL** - A link to a website / landing page
**Hyperlink** - A link to a website or landing page included in your copy
**Landing Page** - A one-page website
**On-Boarding** - The process of welcoming a new customer
**Evergreen** - Content that doesn't date
**SEO** - Search Engine Optimisation
**Email Service Provider (ESP)** - A company that provides the facility for creating emails
**API Integration** - A piece of code that can be used to add functionality to your website
**Plugins** - Software that can be added to your blog or website

**Domain Name** - The part of a network address that identifies it as belonging to a particular domain.

**Click Through Rate** - The proportion of visitors to a web page who follow a hypertext link to a particular site.

**Open rate** - How often a sent email is opened

# Chapter One

# Planning your journey

**In this chapter**
Every business journey starts with research. Or at least it should but quite often it's overlooked in our haste to move onto the next step.

In this first section of the book, and as part of planning your journey we'll start by looking at the key aspects that you need to have covered before you start to build your business online.

Who knew research could be so much fun?

If you're an existing business, you might be tempted to skip this section - DON'T as I share some top tips for reaching out to your existing customer base.

We'll start with research on your new business idea. I'll share my experience with you, what worked and what didn't and why my original idea for Herding Cats failed at the starting gates. We'll then look at how you can survey your existing audience.

Ready to dive in? Let's do this…..

## Introduction to research

As entrepreneurs, we often have more than one idea floating around in our cluttered brains. The impetus to hit the ground running with your new idea is so strong that you commit time and quite often money to get it off the ground, then look back and wonder why it failed. (I have so many unused domain names it's ridiculous!)

Every time I now have a new idea, even if it's for my existing business I do nothing about it until I've undertaken research.

Do you feel a bit daunted by this? Don't be. It doesn't have to be complicated and there are plenty of online tools that can help you.

Research is so valuable. It provides you with fantastic insights and can be the groundwork for your idea. It can shape and influence your business model and give you a clear direction to take.

### What if you're an existing/established business?

When was the last time you 'checked-in' with your customer base? Are you making assumptions about your market? Industry changes so quickly, what worked or was relevant last year, month or even week may be outdated.

What language is your audience using? Is your tone of voice still relevant? Perhaps more importantly, are the services you're offering still what your target audience want or need?

This is particularly important when it's your own business.

And if you're not winning your share of the market, do you know why? Where once your website may have been generating leads and enquiries, it could well have stopped, again - do you know why?

The best, and most effective way to find out is ask.

## Will your idea work?

When I started Herding Cats Digital, Digital Marketing Made Easy I had no idea if there was a real need for it, after all, there are hundreds if not thousands of other businesses, agencies and online gurus doing what I had in mind - albeit not in exactly the same way but it is a very overcrowded space.

My original idea was a bit vague and fluffy around the edges. I knew I had a lot of knowledge about digital marketing and building a business online, but I wasn't sure where I would fit in the big picture, or what services I would offer.

I had a vague notion that I wanted to create online courses to sell, perhaps offer one to one support and ultimately, I wanted to launch a membership site where entrepreneurs could pay a monthly fee in return for access to monthly masterclasses and online resources.

When I look back at my notes from the early days I cringe at how naive they were but without them, I wouldn't have had a starting point.

I made a long list of the skills and knowledge I had, then tried to create packages around them - WRONG!

I had no idea what people wanted, who my audience was or how I was best placed to serve them. I had to make some assumptions (people wanted to learn new skills) but other than that I was clueless - even though I'd been in the industry for years.

So, I did what I always do when I'm stuck - I drew a mind map.

I started with 'WEBSITE' at the centre and worked outwards from there. I broke down every element you need to build a business online, and after a couple of hours, I had 6 core subjects that I could work with.

Once I had these I used them as the basis for writing my survey questions - more on this later.

## Finding your target audience

BUT I had no idea who my target audience was.
Was it entrepreneurs (too vague)
Was it business owners (same thing as entrepreneurs?)
Was it a gender-specific market I wanted to target?
Was it an industry sector?

I really had no clue, so I turned the question around.

WHO DIDN'T I WANT TO WORK WITH?

There is nothing worse than arriving at your desk on a morning knowing that you have a monotonous or tedious day of work ahead. I knew for sure that I didn't want to work with anyone that would drain me of energy and creativity.

From experience, and as someone who has been self-employed for 10 years I know I've often fallen for 'chasing the money' and taken on work because I needed to, not because I wanted to. And it's hard when you have bills and a mortgage to pay. Keeping cash flow steady and consistent is a challenge in itself. But I recognised that certain types of work weren't good for me, mentally or health wise and I certainly wasn't producing my best results when I did them.

I wanted to move away from the traditional exchange of time for money and fulfil my wish for creating online courses and a passive income.

So, I looked on the internet (Facebook, thank you) and worked out who would have a need to learn Digital Marketing skills, and I joined a few Facebook groups with my target audience in mind (coaches and consultants initially, and other service-based businesses.)
I lurked in there for a few weeks, taking note of the questions being asked and pain points that were being highlighted until I felt I had enough material to start building a few survey questions.

## Using Surveys

There were things I wanted to know for sure;
1. What the participants' business was (Did it appeal to a particular sector?)

2. How long had they been in business? (Was business age/growth stage relevant?)

3. What was holding them back from growing their business online?

I then referred back to my mind map and looked at the 6 core subjects that I'd identified as being able to help with, and for the purpose of the survey I broke it down even further.
For example, I included social media but broke it down into;
- How to use it

- How to create engagement

- How to build followers

And also gave the option of 'other'.
You can view the original survey here >>
https://goo.gl/forms/wBicq9d2wyUCCdNl1

Once I was happy with my questions (done is better than perfect!) I created it in Google Forms and shared the link on my personal Facebook page. Before you recoil in horror there was a really good reason for it! I knew I had a few business connections on there so that would help but yes, it was mostly old school friends and family. I was really careful with how I worded it "Can you help to shape my future?" A bit cheesy I know but it was absolutely true - whatever came back would genuinely shape my business. I also asked for people to share the link.

Although your brother's mate might not be your target audience, his boss might be. Your Great Uncle Jerry might be retired but he still has connections. What's the saying, you're never more than 6 steps away from each other?

I used the groups that I had joined on Facebook too, and if they had a certain day of the week for members to share links I made the most of it. If they didn't then I contacted the group admin and asked if it would be OK to post the link.
Important to note that I didn't offer any kind of bribe or reward for completing the survey as I wanted genuine, honest answers, not just from those that thought they were going to get a reward.

I also didn't use it as a form of data capture (gathering email addresses). There are different views on this but personally, I didn't feel I had a connection with survey respondents and I also couldn't be 100% sure that they were my target market, so my email list would have had a lot of irrelevant email addresses on there. Sure, they could unsubscribe but all I was really interested in at this point were the results. I also kept it anonymous, so I would be sure of complete honesty from the participants.
If you want to add data capture then, by all means, go ahead, but I felt I had more response as I wasn't asking for anything in exchange for their opinion, other than 5 minutes of their time.

Trust me, people guard their email addresses as closely as they do their car keys!

Once I felt I exhausted all the Facebook avenues I cast my net further afield and used Twitter and Linkedin. This was a bit of an unknown quantity as I couldn't target as much as I could on Facebook, but I was cool with that, it would still give me some answers from a diverse range of businesses.
Then the hard part - I willed myself not to look at it for a week. Now we may not know each other but I can assure you, I am nosey and impatient - not a good combination!

Why a week? Well, I felt I needed to step back and let whatever was going to happen, happen. I'd been holding on really tight to my ideas and it was wearing me out. I was exhausted before I'd even started so by letting go and taking a step back I was giving myself some breathing space, and perhaps some time for reflection - something I have NEVER done before. I recognised early on that this would be a marathon, not a sprint, and really, a week isn't that long at all.

Anyway, I digress! After the week was up I had over 200 responses - not bad, and I felt this was a decent enough amount to get a balanced result and give me something to work with.

The results really surprised me! I reveal all in the next section.

## Using the survey results

The results weren't what I expected at all, and I was relieved that I'd decided to do a survey before launching anything. It would have failed somewhat spectacularly based on my own assumptions.

Over 60% of the businesses that completed the survey were under 2 years old

Now this was important and could possibly be my ideal client and target market.

55% would join a free online community.

(I included this question as I had the plan to open a free Facebook Group initially).

52.4% would prefer to buy a course rather than join a membership site.

Cue major sulk from me as I REALLY wanted a membership site!

I had my answer. A membership site probably wouldn't work in the early stages, so I parked that idea for the moment and focused on what people DID want - online courses that they can buy as and when they need them, with support from a free online community.

HALLELUJAH - I had the start of a business model, along with a breakdown of what people wanted to learn.

If you're on the Herding Cats mailing list or part of the Facebook group, then you'll know I'm a bit obsessed with surveys!

Even though Herding Cats is relatively young I still like to keep in touch with what's going on, what my audience is looking for and how I can best serve them. I send out an annual survey, and also regularly post 2 or 3 question surveys on social media each month. It's a way of keeping my finger on the pulse of my business and in touch with my audience needs.

**Existing / Established businesses need surveys too**
If you've been in business for a while, then you will have a list of past clients that have worked with you in one capacity or another. That's ready-made survey potential right there. It doesn't matter if it was a while ago that you worked with them. They had a need for your service once upon a time and if they haven't used you again, this is the perfect opportunity to find out why.

Perhaps your systems aren't as up to date as they needed them to be.

It could be price, or that the service package you offered them was outdated when compared to the competition.
You never know, it could be that they've forgotten about you and you might just pick up some extra work by reaching out to them and reminding them that you're there!

In my experience, no one minds being surveyed - it's a chance to have a cuppa and a bit of break whilst legitimately 'working'.

## Using your competition

It's OK to spy on your competitors - in fact, I positively encourage it!

As part of your initial research, identify your top 5 competitors. Take a look at their website and their social media profiles. Look at who's following them (it's OK, they won't know). Chances are they will be part of your target audience too - go ahead and follow them but the main reason for doing this is to look at the content your competitors are posting, and the conversations they are having. This will give you an indication of the pain points that your target market has, which you can use further down the line.

Use hashtags to find topics that you may be able to help with and start creating a list of possible future content for your blog posts.

Look at the profiles of the followers, what are the common factors? Is it the industry sector? Is it a business type?

Use all of this information to gradually build a profile picture of an ideal client and target market.

## Let's talk about prices

It's entirely up to you whether you ask people what price they would pay for your services as part of your survey. I stayed away from it, to be honest as it can open up a can of worms.
I would suggest pricing your services based on your time, skill and knowledge and maybe the industry that you're in. If you start asking what people would be prepared to pay you can bet that they will nearly always go for the cheapest option, and should you then approach them at the a later date they can throw this back at you. This also ties in with my data capture point earlier. You have absolutely no connection (yet) to the survey respondent, so why should they a) give you their email address b) pay for a service from someone they don't yet know.

Besides, have faith in yourself and your services. You're bloody good at what you do - perhaps the best in your field, you should charge accordingly.

## TOP TIPS for every survey

- Make the survey as easy to answer as possible, limit it to 2 or 3 tick box choices.

- ALWAYS add 'other' as an option so they can add their own answer

- Keep your survey short - 10 questions at most so make them work for you

- Use a universal tool that people don't need to create an account or register for. Google Forms is great or there are paid options such as Typeform and SurveyMonkey.

- Let them know how long it will take to complete it

- DON'T incentivise it, you want honest, genuine answers, not those that are in it for the free stuff.

If you used your survey to uncover teaching modules or what service packages to offer, then use the information you've gathered to shape everything. From writing your website copy, to blog post ideas you now have a wealth of information at your fingertips that you can use rather than taking educated guesses.

## Action Steps
- Create a mind map around your skill set
- Consider who your target audience might be
- Create and craft your survey questions
- Use the results to build your business model

# Chapter Two

# Finding Your Market

In this chapter
Building an audience is at the crux of all your digital marketing efforts, and it's possibly one of the most challenging aspects. That applies whether you're new to business or if you've been established for a while.
In this chapter we'll be drilling down into the detail of who you are looking to target with your digital marketing, how to reach them and build an audience along with how to start building those all-important relationships.

Your audience will ultimately become your biggest fans, cheerleaders and flag wavers. They will be your first buyers and the ones that refer business to you so targeting the right audience is super important.

Remember, this is a marathon not a sprint and I can't emphasise enough that it takes patience, consistency and effort. Building an audience won't happen overnight, and it takes focused effort, especially in the online space where people's intentions for being online in the first place may not be to sign up for the latest new thing or make new friends! In this first instance, it's not even a case of them finding you - you need to find them and meet them where they are.

Don't get disillusioned or be put off by that - it is absolutely doable and possible but set your expectations from the outset. I've mentioned before how impatient I am, but I also know that committing to a process takes time but that the rewards are most definitely worth the wait.
By the end of this chapter you will be super focused on who you're targeting and have a plan for moving forward.

I just want to take a moment to clarify some terminology before we dive in so forgive me if this is teaching you to suck eggs but bear with me. These are included in the glossary at the beginning of this book but as I use them quite a lot in this chapter I thought it wise to include them here too.

### Target Audience / Market
This refers to the market you're looking to serve as a whole. So for example if you're a bookkeeper you might want to specialise in helping businesses in the creative sector.
The creative sector is your target market.

### Ideal client / customer
This is the individual person you want to work with. So, if you're looking to work with businesses in the creative sector you need to build a really clear picture of the person you want to target.

From your earlier research you should have built a broad picture of where your services fit and have worked out who they appeal to. It's now time to pull all of that information together and build a clear picture.

You can then niche down even further; graphic designers, web developers, marketing strategists.

## Build a picture

Here is where you get laser focused on who you're targeting. There's a lot to be said for 'niching down' within your target market. In his latest book 'This is Marketing', marketing guru Seth Godin absolutely advocates focusing on a small corner of your market,

*"Find a corner of the market that can't wait for your attention. Go to their extremes. Find a position on the map where you and you alone have the perfect answer."*

If you target everyone, you'll attract no one. Your aim is too wide. Refer back to your research and look for the common denominators. They should stand out, but it some cases it might not be blindingly obvious.

With Herding Cats, I had 2 potential Target Markets; coaches and consultants. When I investigated this market a little deeper (spying on the competition!) I noticed that many coaches had been in business for a while but in the last 2 years had decided to take their business online and were looking for ways to grow. They had the drive and ambition to embrace new ways of marketing but were unsure of the steps they needed to take so were looking for help or guidance.
Using this information, I was able to build a picture.

Gender: Primarily female
Approx Age: Mid 30's to early 50's
Marital Status: Single
Career: Qualified Life coach, NLP Practitioner
Favourite online hang out: Facebook and Instagram
Current pain points: Overwhelm at building their business online

Now it's your turn. Don't worry If you haven't sent your survey out yet or if you've only done a little research. Do this exercise now, then repeat it once you've completed your research. And be prepared to be flexible and adapt. My initial picture was a million miles away from what I thought, but rather than persist and make my services fit an audience I imagined, I pivoted and adapted.

Once you've nailed the basics above, you can then drill even deeper into the detail. As before, try answering these questions now, then compare them to your research results.

1. Why would they have a need for your services?
2. How does it fit in with their business need / situation?
3. What are their goals / motivations for buying your services?
4. How do they access information i.e online/offline, newspapers, books, magazines, social media?
5. What's their pre-selected buying criteria i.e quality, price, reputation or a mixture?

If it helps, give your ideal client a name, you can even cut out a picture from a magazine or find something online that represents them. Every time you make a decision, create a piece of content, develop a new service, ask yourself;
Is this what xxxx would want?
What painpoint does this solve for xxxx?
Would xxxx understand or use this?

## Build an audience
"Build it, they will come"

No, they won't - sorry to break it to you, but I figure you knew that.

You can't expect to start building your business, generating leads and sales if you have no audience - common sense, right? It does sound pretty obvious, but it amazes me how people focus on building their websites then sit back and wait for it to become a money-making machine. Sure, with a solid SEO strategy in place you can get ranked by the search engines and hopefully people will find you, but if you have an audience in place ahead of your launch it gives you something to shout about, something to talk to them about - you can even survey them ahead of launch (see, survey mad!).
One thing you need to understand is that there are different types of audiences online that broadly break into 3 different categories; passive, engaged and advocates or P.E.A.

Let's take a close look at each one and how they fit into your audience building strategy.

## P - Passive
These are the lurkers. The online users that will see your posts, may occasionally engage but for the most part they're there to browse, catch up with news, their friends and check out the latest Instagram posts.

Your content game will need to be strong to stop them scrolling past and grab their attention. When you're building your audience, the Passives aren't your focus so be careful not to get sucked in by them if they 'like' every single piece of content or status update that you post. Having said that, don't dismiss them, block them or ignore them completely. It could be that one day they will be looking for your services, but initially remember that they are not your focus.

**E - Engaged**
We love Engaged users. These are parts of your audience that regularly engage with your content. They comment, like and share your stuff, show up to your online workshops and willingly become part of your email list. They are often ripe for conversion (into a sale) and need to be nurtured through your sales funnel (more on this later).

The trouble with some engaged users when you're just starting out is that they are often times your mum, cousin or other family members and whilst they think they're helping, potentially they're not. If that's the case, have a gentle word and explain what you're hoping to achieve, thank them profusely for their support but ask them to stop with the commenting! Tough, but do you want to grow your business or not?

Genuine engaged users are easy to spot, and you need to get them on your email list or start a conversation with them early on.

When I launched the Digital Marketing Made Easy Facebook group I faced both kinds of engaged audiences, so I speak from experience! One group member in particular was always the first in the queue when it came to accessing free workshops, downloads and masterclasses.

The minute I launched a course to buy, they disappeared in a cloud of dust.

Now this annoyed me, and I could easily have dismissed them or even blocked them from the group, but I thought about it and realised that I didn't know anything about them. I had no idea what their business was (their website and messages were really confused), where they were at in their business journey or what their potential needs were.

So, I reached out to them. I contacted them via Messenger and asked if they would like to have a free 20-minute chat. During the call I asked how I could support them and uncovered some pain points that I absolutely had the solutions for. My next challenge was getting them to buy something. But I didn't need to. At the very end of the conversation they thanked me for the call and the advice, and mentioned that they had taken a look at my online courses, but they felt they needed additional support rather than going it alone, did I offer that too?

This was something of a revelation to me in all honesty but what they said made perfect sense. Much of my engaged audience were at the early stages of their digital journey and whilst the courses were comprehensive, what my audience needed was additional support.

So guess what? I asked the question in the next newsletter I sent to my mailing list as well as in the Facebook group and it was a resounding Yes to additional support. BINGO!

No word of a lie - sales of my courses have trebled as a result!

Pay attention to your engaged users - they can be wealth of knowledge.

**A - Advocates**
Once engaged users have been through your sales funnels the aim is to get them to become Advocates.

Advocates are wonderful, and potentially your biggest source of business. They'll rave about you, talk about you, blog about you and wax lyrical to all about how you saved them from hours of stress and frustration, or whatever issue it is you have solved for them.

Look after these and look after them well. Send a handwritten thank you card if they refer you. Publicly thank them if they give you a testimonial or review and use them as a case study to further your growth.

## Where to find your audience

Now we know the different types of audiences, it's time to start working on ways to attract your target market to you.
You've built a picture based on your research and the survey results. You may already have an inkling as to where they 'hang out' online, and you can test this theory by creating content.

Think of the pain points you uncovered throughout your research, and how you can solve them. Your content could be blog posts offering solutions, social media updates asking further questions, short polls across different channels that require short answers or point towards a solution.

Don't worry about the numbers! Even if you only have 100 followers (or fewer) on each channel you should still test and measure. As your audience grows (which it will if you're consistent) you can revisit this content, rework it and test it again.

I had a gut feeling that my target audience would be on Facebook, so I created a series of blog posts on my website based on solutions to some of the pain points I'd uncovered. I shared the posts on Facebook - either the links or a long form post to see what response they had. I took key elements of the blog post content and created graphics to post on Instagram and Pinterest as well as tweeting out the blog post link on Twitter and sharing on Linkedin.

I did this consistently for about 4 weeks, then I watched the analytics and the results of the posts. It was clear that Facebook was going to be where I should focus my attention as this had the highest interaction and resulted in the most visits back to my website. Whilst I gathered tons of likes on Instagram I could sense these were from a Passive audience. Pinterest did drive traffic back to my website but not on a huge scale, so I knew not to focus too much of my time on there. I was surprised with how much Twitter worked for me at driving traffic, and Linkedin was also up there.

Testing and measuring in this way should become part of your monthly review strategy as social media algorithms change so fast and often overnight so making sure your content is still relevant is super important.

Try it for a month (longer if possible) and see what the results tell you.

Don't let this part of your journey overwhelm you. There are plenty of scheduling tools out there that will allow you to pre-schedule your content. I've included a list of online resources for images, design and scheduling at the end of this chapter.

As much as you're watching and waiting to see where your audience is, you should also make the time to engage. Acknowledge new followers, go through their content and like or share relevant content as well as leaving comments. And if they comment on your stuff, be sure to thank them.

### Focus on the one that works

Once you've nailed down where your audience is, focus on that channel. Don't try to be all things to all people.

If Facebook works best for you put all your time and effort into Facebook. Maybe keep a hand in with other channels but automate the others as much as possible.

If Instagram's your thing, get to be the best damn Instagrammer around.

If it's Pinterest - be the very best you can be.

If you spread yourself too thin you will only reach overwhelm and feel like you're constantly on the hamster wheel of content creation and this will lead to burn out.

Focusing on the platform where your audience is, and that works for you, will also pay dividends further down the line.

Don't worry, you won't be spending all your time on social media, this is just the start of your digital journey.

## Using analytics to find your audience

If you're not familiar with using analytics, now is the time to acquaint yourself with these valuable resources.

### Facebook Insights

Facebook offers a ridiculous amount of really valuable insights into your audience; demographics, content, reach, page views. Use this information to create future posts and content.

Nearly all of the social media platforms offer insights and analytics so start to get familiar with them and make sure you build them into your monthly review strategy.

### Google Analytics

Possibly the most comprehensive, easy to use tool out there. If you haven't installed Google analytics on your website, blog or landing page then you need to make this a priority as you build your audience.

## Building Relationships Part 1

I've purposely split this into 2 parts as it will be an ongoing feature throughout your digital journey, and the relationships you build at this stage will differ from those that you build when you're further along on the road.

Once you start to build your audience, it's time to start looking at building relationships in other ways. These relationships may not be directly with your target audience or ideal client.

When I launched the Digital Marketing Made Easy Facebook Group, I initially wanted to keep it relatively small so that I could really get to know the group members. I offered a free 30-minute Zoom chat to everyone and quite a few took me up on it - it's amazing how connected you feel once you've actually spoken to them 1:1.

## Relationships with your target audience

In the early stages make a point of going back to each new fan or follower and saying hello, thank them for their support and ask how you might be able to help them, or simply let them know that you're available to answer any questions they might have.

You might pick up a few 'spam' followers, so weed these out (a quick look at their profile usually tells you!) and only respond to the ones that match your target market or ideal customer.

Make a point of doing this every day. Whilst you're having your morning cuppa or at the end of the day as you're winding down just spend 10 minutes flicking through your social channels (particularly the one you've decided to focus on) and make the connection.

Also, share and comment on their posts if it genuinely interests you.

It can be so tempting to hide behind your keyboard but you need to put yourself out there and there is nothing like an actual, real life conversation to really get to know someone.
I've seen online gurus approach relationship building in different ways, some are really aggressive and proactive and reach out to everyone who likes or comments on their posts with an option for a 1:1 call instantly. If you're comfortable with this approach, then go for it but ultimately you have to do what works for you.

We're all familiar with the saying that 'people buy from people' and that's as true online as it is offline.

Back in the early days of building my magazine I networked like a crazy person - to the point where I was finalist in 'Networking Woman of the Year'. I was literally everywhere and turned up to every single networking event that came my way. It was said that I would turn up at the opening of an envelope and that's probably true!

I needed to though, I was straight out of the corporate world, I had no business contacts and I knew I had to get my name out there. I joined BNI, 4Networking, Business for Breakfast - I invested every penny I had in growing my network.

Would I do that now? No, in all honesty. Quite often I don't even leave my Shed but still have valuable conversations online every single day. It's so much easier (and cost effective) to jump on a Zoom or Skype chat and you're not limited to your local area.

Also, I'm much pickier today about who I share my time with. I don't want to meet for a 'coffee' and spend ages chasing dead ends. I want to build meaningful relationships with people that have the same values and ethics, have conversations that are mutually beneficial.

And maybe it's the British in me but being too 'in your face' can be very off putting!

Develop a process for how you're going to connect with people and reach out to them.

## Relationships with other experts

I'm a big fan of collaboration, and I'm always reaching out to connect with people that complement what I do. It could be that they are Digital Marketers but that they specialise in one particular area such as SEO - something I know the basics of but am by no means an expert. By connecting with them, commenting on their posts, listening to their podcast and perhaps joining their Facebook group I could see if they held similar values to me, had a similar mission and a similar target audience. If so, then I'd reach out to them. A quick introduction email or a short message via Facebook Messenger works really well. I just introduce myself, tell them why I was reaching out and ask if they are up for a chat to explore ways of how we might be able to work together; guest blogs, podcast guest, Masterclasses. Each time, they said yes and it worked wonderfully well.

There has to be an advantage to both parties for this to work well. The chance for both of you to reach new audiences and leverage your brand being the obvious one. There's also the opportunity for referrals and recommendations.

As your business and influence grows you'll find that people often reach out and ask you to appear as a guest expert. Just make sure you have the same values and how you will promote or support each other ahead of any interview is agreed etc.

Develop a process for how you're going to connect with people and reach out to them.

## Relationships with other experts

I'm a big fan of collaboration, and I'm always reaching out to connect with people that complement what I do. It could be that they are Digital Marketers but that they specialise in one particular area such as SEO - something I know the basics of but am by no means an expert. By connecting with them, commenting on their posts, listening to their podcast and perhaps joining their Facebook group I could see if they held similar values to me, had a similar mission and a similar target audience. If so, then I'd reach out to them. A quick introduction email or a short message via Facebook Messenger works really well. I just introduce myself, tell them why I was reaching out and ask if they are up for a chat to explore ways of how we might be able to work together; guest blogs, podcast guest, Masterclasses. Each time, they said yes and it worked wonderfully well.

There has to be an advantage to both parties for this to work well. The chance for both of you to reach new audiences and leverage your brand being the obvious one. There's also the opportunity for referrals and recommendations.

As your business and influence grows you'll find that people often reach out and ask you to appear as a guest expert. Just make sure you have the same values and how you will promote or support each other ahead of any interview is agreed etc.

Action Steps
- Take some time to drill down into who your target market is - niche down as much as you can.
- Build a vivid picture of your ideal client
- Start to work on building your audience
    - Where are they?
    - Use analytics to help you
- Start to build a relationship with your audience
- Think of other experts whose audience you can tap into through collaboration
- Test and measure your content to engage your audience and find out where engaged users are online
- Develop a process for how you're going to connect with people and reach out to them

**Resources - Social Media Scheduling Tools**
All of these have a free and paid for version.
Hootsuite
Later.com
Buffer

# Chapter Three

# Building Know, Like and Trust

**In this chapter**
We mentioned in the last chapter the importance of building relationships. In this chapter we're going to build on that and show you how to develop relationships built on Know, Like and Trust.

Building Know, Like and Trust is as important online as it is offline, if not more so.

When people are online they're often wary, cautious and resistant to dubious sales tactics. They may have had their fingers burnt before, which makes our job as marketers and business owners even harder.

But we now have so many opportunities for stepping out from behind our keyboards and engaging with our audience; video, podcasts, Facebook Lives, Instagram stories, Snapchat. we are blessed with so much technology (or cursed depending on your view!).

Each one of these platforms is perfect for you to build KLT with your audience but I'm not saying you HAVE to do every activity. Start with what you're comfortable with, blogging for example then push outside of your comfort zone a little and make a video. Test and measure the response, see what works and focus on that format to engage with your audience.
The biggest piece of advice I could give you is to be human, have human conversations, show your flaws and imperfections, your screw ups but also celebrate your wins and successes. People buy from people and showing that you're perfectly normal is absolutely fine.

Let's take a look at each one and share some tactics on how you can win your audience over.

## Understanding the customer journey

Before we delve into the detail, it's worth taking a look at how KLT fits in with the journey that your customer will take towards a buying decision.

We're all aware that how people buy has changed, that they have so much more choice and many options open to them so keeping your brand front and centre of their journey will help with their decision making.

KNOW - Once your customer has established a need they will search online - this could be the first interaction they have with you and your brand.

LIKE - When they land on your website they'll be looking for familiar pages; product/services page, your about page and testimonials from your previous customers, and possibly a free sample (more on this later).

TRUST - Once they've checked out the price, they'll read about you and go straight into the reviews and testimonials - they want proof and affirmation that they're making the right purchasing decision and the best way to do this is from people who have already purchased your services.
Once they've done all that they'll buy from you.

That was easy wasn't it? End of book - you know everything you need to know!

Except..
It's not that easy is it? While that's the theorised journey your potential customer may take, in reality it's very different.
It takes longer for a start.
And more than one view of your brand, more than one interaction with you and definitely more than one view of your services.

Remember, 95% of your marketing activity should be around relationship building, only 5% will be focused on selling - so make it count!

What can you do to heighten the chances of someone buying from you?

**Let's start with Know.**

If you're an extrovert you may not struggle with this, but if you're an introvert it can really push you outside of your comfort zone. You have to let people in and let them get to know you. I'm not saying share your deepest, darkest secret with them, but share enough so that they see behind the social media profile.

Be authentic with your interactions and keep it real. Be nice, offer help, answer questions, make nothing too much trouble but most importantly stay visible. If you've done your earlier research you'll have nailed down where your audience is so show up there and stay relevant and relatable. It could be something as simple as showing your working space, your morning ritual or even what coffee you drink. As long as it's genuine it doesn't matter, just show up and share.

**Like**
Not everyone is going to like you. Sorry, but that's just humans for you. I heard recently that you simply have to divide people's opinions of you - be more Marmite. Bland and uninteresting doesn't stand out, you'll get lost in the noise.

That's bullshit.

If you're creating the right content, for the right people, consistently and with your audience needs first then you will gather your tribe around you with authenticity and they will truly like you for being you.

Use wording in your copy that your audience can relate to, avoid jargon and try to write as you speak. Use humour, quirky images, inspire people and make them feel good about themselves.

Share your values, your vision, your mission. Establish common interests that serve your audience - there's nothing like a sense of familiarity to strengthen the bond.

**Trust**

The best way to build trust with your audience is by being accessible. Make sure your contact details are easily available and answer questions fully. Also, consistency is vital. Show up when you say you're going to - if you have a Facebook live scheduled, make sure you do it. If you publish a podcast every Thursday stay consistent with it. No one is going to buy from you if you're there one week and not the next.

Once you're off the ground ask for testimonials that you can use on your website and in social media posts to build social proof. People want validation that purchasing from you is the right thing to do and that you'll deliver what you have promised.

Don't hesitate to share a success story - if a customer has worked with you and had a major breakthrough, write about it. Create case studies, share the outcome and what happened as a result of working with you.

If you weave each element into your content, consistently then you will develop know, like and trust with your audience. Remember, this isn't about sales, this is about building the blocks for your brand and your business.

## Build KLT by providing value

Yep, we're STILL not selling anything. Yet!
We started this chapter by spelling out the customer journey, and there's one important element that you need that cements the know, like and trust formula; the chance for someone to experience your services without making a commitment to buy anything.
You may have heard this called a free download, a lead magnet or an opt-in bribe. You are basically exchanging free information in exchange for their email address.
But what? And why?
What you provide them with is entirely dependent on your business, but it should always be solution focused. I'll dig a bit deeper into the What in the next section - for now let's focus on the Why.

Once a potential customer hits your website as part of their decision-making process they want you to demonstrate to them that you know what you're talking about.

They will have seen you on social media, perhaps read some of your blog posts, you may even have had a small interaction with them. However, they have found you, they want to know more.

Providing a free sample is the perfect way of doing this.
This free sample more often than not takes the shape of a free download that provides part of the solution to the problem that they face or the need that they have.
It doesn't have to be long or overcomplicated. A simple PDF download, a workbook, a video series - as long as it solves or goes some of the way to solving their problem.
This is your chance to demonstrate your skills, knowledge and expertise.

Think back to your earlier research and the pain points that you uncovered. What can you create that will be compelling enough for someone to give you their email address?
This is the first step in building your email list.

## KLT & Sales

Here's the odd thing about marketing your business online. If you move in for the sale too soon, you'll lose the crowd.

Think of it like a comedian delivering the punchline of a joke without any of the background or build up. The audience will be bewildered, confused and quite possibly walk out.

They'll wonder why they bought a ticket in the first place, and chances are they will slate the comedian to friends and family and before you know it - end of comedian's career.

Sounds drastic right? Trust me, try and sell too soon online and you'll fall at the first hurdle. The online world can be brutal that's for sure but there's plenty that you can do to ensure this never happens to you.

Your first step is to build know, like, trust;
Share stories
Be human and authentic
Establish common ground
Ask for and share testimonials
This is all very well I hear you cry but exactly when do I start to actually make any money? Well, I'm getting to that, but all of these steps are an absolutely crucial part of your digital journey.

### Action Steps

- Be yourself, warts and all
- Map out the journey your customer will take to find you
- Show up and be consistent

# Chapter Four

# List Building Made Easy

**In this chapter**
In this chapter we'll uncover why capturing email addresses is so important to your digital marketing success, and how you can use them as part of your sales funnel to develop a deeper connection with your audience that you can then nurture a relationship with and gently guide them towards being your biggest fans.

It's often considered the Holy Grail of Digital Marketing success, and though in some circumstances it can be an overused concept, if you do it right, it really can be pivotal in your success.

We'll uncover why people protect their email addresses so carefully and how you can overcome this using genuine methods of data capture.

We'll also look at some of the core ingredients you need in your list building strategy, the different list building techniques and how to create your first free download. We'll then look at how you can use your copy to make it more enticing for your audience to share their email address with you to access your free download.

## Part One - What is List Building?

How would it feel to have a ready-made audience ready to buy your services, products or courses?

How about being able to ask for feedback even BEFORE you launch a new product, service or course?

How easier would your life be if you had cultivated an audience that you had built a rapport with? That already see you as a trusted source of information?

How much FUN would it be to have your audience highly engaged and just waiting for your latest new thing?

That, in a nutshell is what list building is all about.

Now, you may have heard 'the money is in the list' and been aware that email addresses are important, but you've been turned off simply because your own inbox is full of spam, junk and generally useless information that you're not even sure when or how you signed up for. (If that is the case use a tool like Sanebox to have a clean-up).

But how would it be if you subscribed to something that provided real value? Whose email you instantly opened every time it landed in your inbox because you knew they wouldn't email you if they had nothing of value to add to your world? This is the kind of list building I'm talking about.

Before we really get under the skin of this I feel that I need to bust a few myths.

- Building an email list will not happen overnight
- You will not be a 6-figure earner in the space of 24 hours
- Building your email list is hard work, takes time and infinite amounts of patience

It probably is possible to achieve all of these things if you have an unlimited advertising spend and an already established presence but as you're reading this book I'm guessing you're not in that place just yet.

As you're probably aware by now, digital marketing is all about the long game and even if you've spent time building your social media audience and possibly your website traffic, algorithms on both can sometimes change overnight and where you once had hundreds if not thousands of followers and fans, you could potentially be left with nothing - or very little.

How would you communicate with these people again? How do you get back in touch with them?

And knowing what you now know about how transient the online world can be, do you have the patience and time to start again?

No, thought not.

This is why capturing email addresses is a crucial part of your digital marketing strategy.

Not just that, but once someone has trusted you enough to share their email address with you it also means that you can now start to build a deeper relationship on a more permanent basis.

No more relying on pesky algorithms and instead having a ready-made audience - who wouldn't want that?
We're going to dig really deep into this a bit further on, but it's important that you understand the WHY before we move onto the WHAT and the HOW.

## Part Two - List Building Made Easy

Let me just say at this point, that you DON'T have to give something away - you could add a simple sign up form to your website asking people to subscribe to your newsletter - that's absolutely fine, just make it an enticing message instead of 'Subscribe Here', no one really wants to subscribe to anything!

Here are a few alternative examples;
"Keep up to date with all the latest on XYZ"
"Want the low down on XYZ delivered every week?"
"Don't miss out on discounts and free samples"

One of the most popular formats for building your email list is by providing a free sample / taste of you, your business, your knowledge and expertise.

Remember that as part of the customer journey potential customers will 'shop' around? What if your website / landing page offered a solution to their pain point for free?

List Building Made Easy was the title for one of my successful free downloads, it's also been the topic of Masterclasses delivered in Facebook Groups, at networking events and has featured across the internet on various sites such as Medium.com

Why was it so successful? Because every business owner in whatever field is always struggling to find the golden nugget that will allow them to build their email list quickly and easily.

Except, as I mentioned in the introduction - building your email list takes time, effort and patience and here was a free download that covered all the essential steps to get you started, without the overwhelming, complicated process.

So now we've established the importance of building your list, let's really get under the skin and look at the What and the How.

We've already touched on building your list by adding value, so let's look at what you could create.

This will form the basis for your free opt-in.

But let's address the elephant in the room, shall we? Why the hell are you giving away the solution for free when you're in business to make money?

OK, this is something that crops up all the time. Here's the thing;

*You are only providing 20% of the solution with your free download. The 80% is what they pay for.*

Take my first workbook that I mentioned earlier 'List Building Made Easy'. I had identified that one of the main pain points my target market faced was building their business online. Without an email list it's practically impossible to achieve most business outcomes. WOW that's a huge claim, and I'm sure there are people that would disagree, and maybe prove me wrong but for the ordinary Joe Soap entrepreneur it's bloody hard!

So once I'd identified a pain point I drilled a little further into the detail and discovered that most entrepreneurs actually did understand the need for an email list, knew the components involved and were willing for the most part to do it for themselves - my workbook went 20% of the way to helping them achieve that.
I broke it down into steps (similar to how this book works) and gave them space to work out the How, with pointers from me.

What it didn't do was build the relevant platforms for them. It did however include a Call To Action mentioning that I offered a Done For You service whereby I could build the platforms FOR them, then hand it over all completed - they then just needed to promote it and start gathering email addresses.

I had relative success with this, but the word of mouth referrals were exceptional. Simply because I gave people the option meant that I had achieved 2 things. I had built my own email list of potential customers, but I also had a platform to upsell and convert them directly into customers who then raved about my services.

I went ALL OUT to over service these few initial customers so that I could gather feedback, testimonials and social proof that I was able to use further down the line. This is something I absolutely encourage you to do too - it pays in the long run.
Let's have a look at the different types of list building techniques.

The first (and most obvious) place to start is with your website.

**On your blog**
Include a simple subscribe button within your blog page so that people can subscribe to the latest updates. Every time you publish a new blog post your subscribers will be notified and as a result you'll get more eyeballs on your blog post.
On the blog post itself include a call to action that directs readers to your free opt-in too. If they're interested enough to read your content, then you're halfway there.

**On your About page**
Again, add a simple form to your About page, it's one of the most viewed pages on any website so simply ask them to sign up to your newsletter, or if you've highlighted a pain point in your copy offer them the solution by including the link to your free opt-in.

**On your Home page**
Either in your header (the area at the top of your website) or in the footer include a call to action encouraging people to subscribe. Give them little hints about what they will receive if they sign up - focus on the benefits and let them know how often you'll write to them.

## On Social Media

All social media profiles include an area where you can add a URL - sometimes more than one. If it's restricted to one (such as Instagram) you can use a tool such as Linktre.com which allows you to create multiple links - or if you're really clever you can create a hidden page on your website that contains all the links, but you might want to ask your web designer about that one!
I regularly change the URL in line with whatever course or Masterclass that I'm promoting that month.

## Collaboration

Do you know someone else in business that complements yours? For example, if you're a jewellery designer, do you know a wedding photographer? If so, and they have a blog, can you write a Guest Post for them? This is a great way to build your audience and your email list at the same time.

If you think a little deeper about a partnership or collaboration, is there something you can create together that benefits both of your audiences? Such as an eBook or joint Whitepaper on a particular topic? By promoting it to a wider audience you'll increase your reach, presence and authority which will in turn increase your visibility and sign ups.

## Existing Email List

If you have an existing list that maybe you haven't reached out to for a time, send an email asking them to re opt-in. This is something that should have been done in conjunction with the new GDPR rules that came into effect in May 2018, but it's never too late.

If you do this and some people don't respond, then ditch them! It may seem counterintuitive, but you don't want people on your list just for the sake of the numbers. You only want those that are engaged and interested in what you have to offer.

## Email Signature
Add a simple hyperlink at the bottom of your email signature strip. Think about the amount of emails you send out every day, and how many of these people are your potential customers. You're not being overly pushy, just simply asking them to keep up to date with the latest news from you - easy.

So now you have some ideas of the different places you start to build your email list, let's take a look at some other tools you can use to help you.

## Pop up box
Love 'em or hate 'em pop up boxes on your website or blog are the most effective way of building your email list. The secret to making them successful for you is all down to the timing. If you set a popup to display within seconds of someone landing on your site it can be a total turn off. I mean, I've only just discovered you, I don't know anything about you, I don't know what you do, what you offer or how you could add value so why would I want to subscribe to something else when my inbox is already full?

Depending on the tool you use (I use Sumo) you can select when the popup should display and also the look and feel of it. There are many tools out there but I find Sumo the easiest to use and it looks great, but you can also use Mailchimp, which is free up to 2,000 subscribers and very easy to install.

## Dedicated Landing Page
This landing page has one job - to capture email addresses. Don't let it get overcrowded with content and only have one call to action - submit your email address! We'll discuss this in Chapter Five.

## Creating Your Offer
Now we're getting into the nuts and bolts of List Building Made Easy!

## Finding Topic Ideas for your Opt-In

Take a look at your analytics, on your website and on your social media channels - basically anywhere that you have published content in the last 3 - 6 months. What has been your most popular blog post? What has been the most common Facebook discussion? Which tweet, and which link created the most engagement? That's where you start!

Once you've narrowed it down, think about the most frustrating 'things to do' within your area of expertise. How have you dealt with this? What were the steps you took to get past this sticking point? Could this help someone else?

*Example*
*As a seasoned Freelance Copywriter, I had several tips up my sleeve that could help new copywriters just starting out. I wrote a checklist and shared it on my blog and in my network, with a call to action for the Copywriting Coaching Package that I was offering. My expertise (and days of being broke!) could help others avoid the same pitfalls.*
Perhaps you are a health and wellbeing coach and you're looking to work with busy mums who are pushed for time. What solutions do you have in your set of skills that can help them with their health whilst fitting it into their lifestyle.
Remember you're looking for the pain points of your ideal clients so that you can offer solutions whilst adding value.


## Creating Clickable Headlines

There is literally no end to the free opt-ins that you could create but how you word them, from the headline to the call to action is where the success lies.

Consider this;
A list of 10 diets you could try
Compared to;
10 Proven Diets To Lose Weight Instantly

You'd be more likely to sign up to the one bottom, right?
Think about why that is.
1. 'Proven' means someone else has done the hard work of testing these diets out.

2. 'Lose Weight' is very appealing

3. 'Instantly' - even better

But there are a couple of things to be aware of too.
1. Proven? By who, and what do they know? Why are they the expert?

2. Instantly? Really? Sound too good to be true? Are you selling a false promise?


You really need to dedicate some time to crafting an attention-grabbing headline, but one that will deliver on its promise. If you can include the identified pain point of your potential email subscriber, this creates a hook, something that resonates with them and captures their attention.

A relatively easy one to start with would be a simple 'How To';
How to {solve a problem}
How to X without XYZ e.g How to lose weight without leaving the couch
How to X when XYZ e.g How to shed pounds when you can't be bothered
X Ways to X when you're XYZ e.g 10 Ways to eat out when you're on a diet
Pain point: X tools to XYZ e.g 10 Tools to Help you lose weight
Why you're not X and what to do about it e.g Why you're not losing weight and what to do about it

With all of the above examples you're identifying the pain point and offering a solution. It might not be the whole solution but by sharing your expert knowledge you're setting yourself out as someone who can be trusted, can be seen as an expert and most importantly you're adding value.

Once you're clear on the subject of your free opt-in, it's now time to consider what format it will take.
I would say in the first instance keep it simple, and as your confidence and audience grow you can look to more complex ideas. Here are just a few to start with;

- Top Tips - a simple list of your top ten tips (1-page PDF)
- Free templates
- Worksheets
- eBooks

As you progress you can move onto more in-depth ideas. These may take you a bit longer to create but will provide tons of value;
- X day challenge - a series of automated emails with a different challenge for the subscriber to try each day
- Video series
- Webinar

Hopefully by now you're firing on all cylinders and coming up with ideas for your first free opt-in like a confetti cannon has exploded in your mind!
Before we move on, take some time to ask yourself (and answer!);
- What are you going to create?
- What is the purpose?
- What pain point does it solve?
- What value does it deliver?

In all of this remember; share the WHAT and WHY by adding as much value as you can, make the HOW something they would willingly hand over money for!
I can't stress enough that List Building is a numbers game, the wider your reach and deeper your connection with your audience, the more successful you will be.

REACH + CONNECTION = SUCCESS

It takes time and considerable patience to build your email list so treat each person on your list as your best friend and always keep adding value to their world.

### Top List Building Tips

- Start early, even if you don't have a website create a free landing page using something like Mailchimp and start your list.

- Test and measure - always. Try different headlines, images and CTA's for the same opt in and see which attracts the most sign ups. Only try one thing at a time or you won't know what works!

- Have more than one opt-in - start with one, but as you develop your business and grow your audience create different opt ins for different audiences.

### Action Steps

- Consider how you might start building your email list - a newsletter or a free download?

- Remember, you're only providing 20% of the solution for free

- Look at where you can promote your free download

- Who can you collaborate with to grow your reach and build your email list

- What can you create?

- Brainstorm headlines and keywords to use in your copy

- Play around with the headline to create an enticing hook

**Resources - Creating your free download**
**Free Images:**
Unsplash
Pexel
Pixabay
**Free Design:**
Canva
Pic Mon

# Chapter Five

# Sales Funnels

**In this chapter**
If you're not familiar with the term Sales Funnel, it's a sale and marketing term that describes the journey your potential customer will take on their way to making a buying decision.
We'll update the traditional sales funnel process to incorporate the steps you've taken in building your business so far.

We'll delve deeper into the trust element and how your free download fits into the process.

I've also included a personal case study to demonstrate how a purchasing decision might be made, and why it's NOT always down to price.

We briefly glimpse at what you should do once the sales start and how to turn buyers into raving fans.

**What is a Sales Funnel?**
Traditionally the typical marketing / sales funnel followed the AIDA process; Awareness, Interest, Desire, Action.
The online or digital sales funnel has moved far deeper than that as we have a greater understanding of buyer behaviour online.
We've already talked about Know, Like and Trust and this forms the fundamental basis for an online sales funnel and everything you need is built around this.
If we take that original sales funnel concept of AIDA and work Know, Like and Trust into it we begin to unravel the process.

### Awareness (Know)

Unsurprisingly this is ensuring that your brand is visible to your target market so that they become aware of your existence. In the early days, being active on Social Media is a good way to introduce your brand to potential customers, but also consider PR, advertising (Google Adwords / Facebook Ads) if you have the budget.
Don't hide behind your keyboard, let people get to know you - warts and all!

### Engagement (Like)

If someone responds to a comment, photo, video, blog post engage with them, It could be as simple as saying thank you but starting that conversation is the first step in building engagement and the like factor will follow.

### Interest (Like)

As the prospect moves further along your sales funnel and shows more of an interest make sure your marketing ALWAYS has a call to action. It doesn't have to be in your face BUY NOW (in fact, that's the last thing you should do!) but tell them where you want them to go and what you want them to do when they get there. Make it simple, tell them what you want them to do next.

### Desire (Trust)

So now you've established know and like, and trust is the next step - and it's a biggie.

Building trust with your potential new customer is vital. Start slowly, at first you want to establish that they can trust you with their email address i.e. you're not going to spam the life out of them or fill their inbox with junk that's not relevant. This could be where your free download, free sample or whatever giveaway you decide on can come into play. If you make it enticing enough (you're going to take away their pain point) then they'll willingly share their email address with you.

You should give away just enough for them to want something more - more information, more proof that you're the best value, more understanding of how you work, more confidence that you know what you're talking about and their desire to work with you or buy from is the right choice.

**Decision (Trust)**
Whooaaa, there should almost a step prior to this called 'people are indecisive', let me explain - you've spent what seems like ages building the know, like and trust and now it's down to the prospect to make their decision. Rarely, unless you're a big brand or have thousands to spend on advertising campaigns, are business purchases made on impulse. If your target market hangs out on social media then the likelihood of them making a snap decision to buy from you after the first interaction is unusual. I'm not saying it doesn't happen - maybe if you have a flash sale of one of your courses, or services it could happen but it's unlikely. Before they make a decision, they will search for validation that they are in the right place, with the right person. They will compare reviews, search out testimonials and look for social proof. Once they've satisfied their curiosity only then will they buy.

Think about your own decision making or buying process. How do you decide what to buy and from whom?

As an example, I had an occasion recently to visit the vet with one of my cats. He recommended that she was put on a special diet and gave me the choice of trying a free sample along with a discount if I purchased from them. Now, I knew I could potentially get a better deal online, so I took the free sample and said I would get back to him. Of course, the first thing I did was search for this special diet food online and I had a myriad of choices, all at different price points - some much cheaper than the vet's price. I considered what factors would influence my decision.

I knew the vets, we'd been going there for years.

My cat liked the free sample, and it was a brand I was aware of. Even with the discount voucher the prices online were much cheaper. The following day, having still not made my decision I received an email from the vets (I'd given it to them so I could get the discount voucher), that explained why my cat needed the diet, what the benefits of the diet were but also what the benefits of buying direct from my vets were which included a donation to a local cat charity if I used the voucher within the next 10 days.

Guess what I did? Yes, I bought from the vet even though the price was higher. None of the other websites had offered a donation, and my vet clearly knew my love of cats, so this was the extra bonus that tipped my decision.

But can you see how it followed the principles of know, like and trust?

Not all buying decisions are made on price so what can you do to make that decision easier for your prospect? Keep it simple but make it non-negotiable for them to buy anywhere else!

**Nurture (Know, Like, Trust)**
Once sales have started to happen, the journey doesn't end there. You have them in your sales funnel and you can now nurture them through to the final stages.
If you're offering a 1:1 service, this is also known as on-boarding. So what happens once a prospect agrees to work with you? What can they expect to happen next?
Remember, people like to be told what to do, and this part of the process is just as important as all the rest. You can create an automated email sequence that directs them to take various actions. Maybe to book a call with you or an area on your website that they need to access to set up an account. It could be to a booking link so that you can have a 1:1 chat with them.

If it's a product or a course they've bought, then what happens next? Do they need an access code, username and password or confirmation for when the course starts?

It can be something as simple as saying 'thank you', share with them how much you appreciate their support but ALWAYS tell them what happens next.

We'll cover the Email nurturing sequence in much further detail in the next chapter but for now, give some thought as to what you can do to reassure your new customer that they've made the right decision.

**Repeat Sales (Trust)**

I like to refer to this section as the 'flag waving'. Once your new customer has made their initial purchase you want them to rave about you, to tell everyone about how great you are, how easy it was to work with you and give you testimonials or even better agree to be part of a case study. Again, this may not happen organically, and they may need a little prompting so make sure you have a place where they can leave a review either on your website (preferably) or on Google or even your Facebook page.

You can even create a Customer Satisfaction survey (yep, still survey mad!) for them to complete. This is possibly the most effective way to gather testimonials as you can reuse their words across social media and also on your website and wherever else you want to wave flags. It's even better if you can encourage them to use their own platforms to flag wave; social proof and a wider audience reach is always a huge bonus.

If you use the survey method, there are 2 important things that you need to include. Firstly, ask for their permission to use it in your marketing but most importantly ask them if they would buy from you again. You can use this statistic in future marketing material, and even create blog posts around the information.

After the initial furore of your success, consider how long it might be before they need your product or service again. Consider setting up an automated email sequence to keep in touch, or make a diary note to contact them again in say 3 months. Gently remind them that you are still there, that they said they would use you again and perhaps offer a loyalty bonus if they buy from you again within a certain timeframe. It's also the perfect opportunity to offer an upsell, but more about that in the next section.

## Building your first sales funnel

By now you should have a good understanding of why you need a sales funnel and the various key elements you need to include to start attracting your target market. In this section we're going to have a brief look at what technical elements you need, how to source them and how to put it all together with as little fuss and technical knowledge as possible.

As a bonus for the buying the book you have free unlimited access to the 'Create a Sales Funnel (in 5 easy steps) course which you can access here.

https://www.herdingcatsdigital.com/bookresources

In the course I cover what I refer to as a Rinse and Repeat sales funnel. It doesn't matter what you are selling, the tools you need are just the same so once you learn the skills you can use over again, maybe tweaking each time based on success.

## Different types of Sales Funnels

You don't need to have an all singing, all dancing website. In fact, you don't need to have a website at all to build your first digital sales funnel. A simple (free) landing page, an email service provider and your first free download are all you initially need.

It can be argued that there are hundreds of different types of sales funnels based on whatever you're selling. Let's keep things simple and look at the main two that you will use when you're just starting out. The principle for both is the same; landing page, opt in, delivery - but one operates without you (Evergreen Funnel) and the other requires more input from you (Launch Funnel).

## Evergreen Sales Funnel

As with every sales funnel, you need the basics in place and depending on your budget there are tons of options out there. I'm going to recommend both free and paid for and these are based on my own experiences and conversion rates.

The Evergreen Sales Funnel is one that runs continuously (the content doesn't date or isn't date/time dependant) and provides you with a continuous revenue stream. You will do all the work up front or in advance, then it will happily work for you in the background with very little input needed on a day to day basis.

To create an Evergreen funnel, you really need to give a lot of thought to what your free opt in will be. If it's a Top Ten tips for example will they date over time? Will new processes or systems come into play that will date your content? A free workbook works really well as an Evergreen opt-in, as long as it ties in with whatever you're selling at the end of the funnel.

For example, for my course 'Create A Sales Funnel (in 5 easy steps)' I created a free workbook that laid out the steps needed to create your own digital road map. Creating a sales funnel was part of that journey and I included a little about the why in the workbook, with the hint that this was a vital step and that I would share more in the coming days.

A couple of days after they received the workbook I sent another email highlighting how important having a sales funnel was and that I would be hosting a webinar on the topic along with a couple of dates and times so people could register.

They received a couple of emails reminding them of the date they had selected and once that day arrived I automatically sent them an email with the link to a pre-recorded webinar that delved deeper into the why and showed a little of the how.

At the end of the webinar I declared that the course was now available to buy using a discount code as a thank you for watching.

Once the webinar was over they then received follow up emails prompting them that the cart would be closing in XYZ days so to act now.

It works wonderfully well and sells the course with only the occasional input from me. I make sure I answer any questions or queries promptly and once the payment has been processed I send a thank you email along with a 'check-in' email every so often to see how they're getting on.

An Evergreen Sales Funnel isn't for everyone but if you're just starting out, trying to grow your email list or introduce your audience to your products or services it can work for you.

**Benefits of an Evergreen Funnel**
One of things I love about an Evergreen Sales Funnel is that it works more or less without you. It can happily run in the background whilst you get on with other things, such as creating new content, growing your business or supporting 1:1 clients.

It also generates that passive income that everyone seems to be striving for. Just a word of caution, the word passive is misleading. You will need to put in a lot of time and effort up front, but it is totally worth the return.
Once you have the fundamental tools in place it's then a case of Rinse & Repeat. All that will need to change is your opt in freebie and your sales messages.

Finally, with an Evergreen Sales Funnel there is no start or end date so your income will be consistent, without having to gear up to a huge launch every quarter and receiving no income in between.

## Drawbacks of an Evergreen Funnel

In the first instance, it's a lot of work and there is a lot to think about which may seem overwhelming and put some people off even starting. Remember though, it's only complex if you make it that way. Using the tools I've suggested above takes away the complexity.

You MUST test test, and test again. EVERY single part of your Evergreen funnel must work seamlessly, from your email sign up form to the payment gateway. Even the slightest hitch, delay or error will turn people off and turn them away without letting you know what went wrong.

(I learnt this the hard way - I incorrectly set up a discount code and it expired earlier than I thought so although there was a flood of traffic after my webinar no one was able to buy at the discounted rate, and NO ONE let me know, they just walked away! I could tell from the analytics that over 50 people wanted to buy at £97 per course - I was gutted!)

Only a very small percentage of your email list will buy from you, it's currently around 3 percent so that means you will constantly be having to drive traffic back to the landing page. The quickest and most effective is through advertising, either Google Adwords or Facebook ads but as the cost for both platforms is rising you must be prepared to allocate a budget of at least £500 per month to see a return of cost per lead at around 30p - 80p per lead.

The beauty of an Evergreen Funnel is the opportunity to test and measure. If sales start to slow (or don't happen) you can revisit every aspect of your funnel and tweak or adjust your messages. Make sure you have analytics installed so you can monitor the traffic, bounce rate, exit pages and drop off rate. Because you're adding new email subscribers to your list all the time they won't know any different so keep tweaking until you hit on the perfect formula.

## The Launch Sales Funnel

A Launch Sales Funnel is one of the most exciting, exhilarating and stressful experiences I have been through! When I first started out this was how I sold my online courses and it was/is exhausting and truly leaves you frazzled by the end of it but OMG what a rush!

Technically, it works the same as the Evergreen Funnel only with a shorter sequence; landing page, email provider and automated delivery, but it requires hands on involvement from you. You may decide to set up a pop up Facebook Group to deliver live Q & As, and your email sequence may be more intense, with more emphasis on scarcity and urgency to buy. Everything you do online for the 8 weeks preceding the 'cart open' will be geared around your launch, and for about 2 weeks after to tie up any loose ends or questions.

A launch funnel runs two, maybe three times a year tops and if you have no other revenue streams your income can be limited, so you need to make sure that the launches are as successful as possible.

**Benefits of a Launch Funnel**
As intense as a launch funnel may be, you only need to do the work once or twice a year. You can run a beta test with 10 or so volunteers prior to a full launch so that you have feedback and social proof from outside that a) it works and b) some stats to throw into your sales messages.
By only making your product/service available a couple of times a year you create FOMO (fear of missing out) and can set up a waitlist for those that didn't get chance to buy first time round. This gives you an indication of how your sales might go in the next launch.

**Drawbacks of a Launch Funnel**
The most obvious one, especially if you're just starting out is that you're only generating revenue two to three times a year so you're relying on each launch to be super successful to stay in business!
If just one of your launches fail, you don't get a chance to tweak and test again until the next time round.

If you use your launch funnel to open doors to a monthly membership site then it's ideal as you will have the recurring revenue from existing members to keep you going, but once again you will have to be constantly building your email list, growing your online presence and authority and making new connections in between launches.

In summary, the key elements of every sales funnel are as follow;

- A landing page (to capture email addresses)

- An email service provider (ESP) to deliver your opt in and subsequent emails

- Automated nurturing sequence leading to your sales pitch

PLUS for an Evergreen Sales Funnel you'll need

- A sales page to deliver your webinar or sales copy

- Countdown timer to create urgency or scarcity

- Shopping cart to collect payment

WOW - that seems a lot and quite overwhelming doesn't it? It doesn't have to be as you'll see once you've watched the course.

The decisions you'll need to make are;

**1. Landing Page**
Where and how will you build your landing page? A landing page is simply a one page website that has one job - to collect email addresses. There are tons of options out there, here are the tools that I use and I state whether it's free or paid for.

**LeadPages** - paid for
I have quite a few LeadPages set up for Evergreen content and it works really with Wordpress or as a standalone. It has integrated analytics and SEO tools which means it gets found easier and appears in search results. Depending on what you're offering there are loads of templates to use as well as the option to completely customise your landing page. LeadPages also offers an automated email delivery service once someone opts in although I found the customisation of this limited. You don't need to have a website to create a LeadPages landing page as it generates URL for you, but it is preferable to have one.

**Mailchimp** - free up to 2k email addresses
Some people are quite sniffy about using Mailchimp but to be honest it's ideal and works really well when you're just starting out. It has a drag and drop editor, so it makes creating a landing page very quick and easy. Mailchimp also acts as an Email Service Provider so there's no need for API integration as you would have with LeadPages for example. You don't need to have a website to use Mailchimp but again it will create a random URL that you can customise.

**PlugIns**
If you have a Wordpress website, then there are tons of options out there to add plugins and easily create a quick landing page. The benefits of this are that you can use your own domain name plus the name of your opt in so it will appear in search results if you do all the surrounding SEO. I have tried loads over the years, but when I was just starting to grow my email list I used Landing Page Cat. It's free with the option to upgrade but I really didn't need to as it served my purpose really well. It's very easy to use, not at all over complicated and has enough levels of customisation that make it quick and easy to put a landing page together in no time. It also integrates seamlessly with Mailchimp which is another huge bonus.

## 2. Automated delivery of your opt-in using an Email Service Provider

As I mentioned above, you can use either LeadPages or Mailchimp for both the landing page and the automated emails.

To keep everything simple and easy to follow I'm going to stick with Mailchimp as it's free and perfect for when you're just starting out.

Again, please refer to the free course 'Create A Sales Funnel (in 5 easy steps) for the 'how' which includes step by step 'live' screen action showing you how to create your first list which is where all of your subscribers will initially go.

The most important action that needs to take place once someone has signed up is the delivery of the free goods. Using Mailchimp's automated email sequence you can create your first email to trigger immediately - as soon as they sign up - so that it's delivered straight away. Remember this is the first step of the sales funnel, and possibly their first real interaction with you so it's important that it's painless, hassle free and immediately accessible. You can include links, files, images or buttons to allow them to access the the goodies but make sure you test, test again and triple test before you make it live. It has to work seamlessly and be effort free.

My advice would be to shop and around and see what works for you but overall, keep it simple and make life easy for yourself. Don't over complicate the process.

Final word; if your sales funnel isn't working you need to be really honest and ask yourself what's wrong. Don't be scared to go back and re-examine every single step and make changes where necessary. If people have signed up and not bought from you don't be afraid to ask them why. This is really useful and insightful feedback that will only make your sales funnel more robust.

## Action Steps
- Decide on which type of sales funnel would work well for you right now
- Decide on a landing page provider
- Decide on an Email Service Provider
- Write the copy for your landing page
- Download and watch the free sales funnel course in conjunction with the advice in this chapter

# Chapter Six

# Email Marketing

**In this chapter**
Email marketing will form a huge part of your digital marketing strategy so it's important that you understand how much of an impact it will make on your business, and ultimately your bottom line.
In this chapter we're going to look at email marketing in depth, how you can use it to nurture your new-found friends (subscribers) along with;

- Segmenting your audience
- Setting goals
- Testing and measuring
- Staying in alignment with your brand
- Keep it compelling
- Take your subscribers on a journey that leads to sales
- Different nurturing sequences

I have used email marketing to grow my business for a number of years and it is the number one source of sales for my digital marketing courses, but this was no accident. I've taken time to build relationships and more importantly, very few of my emails actually talk about sales.

One of the biggest objections I hear from people is that they never know what to say in an email, what to talk about, what to write and especially *how* to write so we'll address that issue as well.
I'll share with you the different nurturing sequences I use depending on how people signed up to my list, and how you can apply them in your business.

The most important thing to remember here is that this is YOUR nurturing sequence, only YOUR words, YOUR stories will do - you can learn tips, tricks and techniques from others, but it needs to translate into your own tone of voice and your style. More on this later.

*"The first marketing email was sent in 1978, resulted in $13 million in sales, and kicked off what has become one of the most highly used marketing channels even to this day. Given its early beginnings, email isn't as shiny as some newer channels like messaging and social, but it is an effective way to build an owned audience that gets results." *Hubspot 2017*

Crazy, right? You would have thought that the rate Digital Marketing progresses some clever bod somewhere would have invented a more comprehensive way of building relationships with your potential customer rather than relying on the written word.

But think about it, even if you're using ChatBots (which are the current trend as this book is being written) you're still relying on written words to get your message across.
If this is an area that you're not confident in then never fear, help is here!

The massive difference with email marketing is that it's permission based. The subscriber has given their permission for you to keep in touch with them. You're not annoying them with out-of-the blue cold calls, and you're not interrupting their day by demanding their presence immediately. With an email they can open it in their own time, when they're ready.
This makes the content of your emails all the more important, and not every single email should be a sale! You should treat each email you send as though you are talking to one person, not 100's.

Your email marketing strategy is an important part of your Digital Road Map, and as such you need to take time to plan your content, consider how you can add value and genuinely help your subscribers achieve their goals.

Email marketing is not about you - it's about your audience.

## Segmenting your Audience

Each time you create a new opt-in, whatever email service provider you are using will require you to either create a new list or segment / tag your new subscribers. Most people overlook this step and either have loads of separate lists or one huge list with everyone lumped together.

When it comes to building a relationship with your new subscribers, having everyone in the same list without distinguishing segments / tags will make your job a whole lot harder and limit the success of any email campaign.

If you segment / tag as each list is built, you will know what they signed up for in the first place and you can continue to communicate with them about that topic.

*Example*

*One of my first free downloads was a simple one-page PDF sharing top tips on how to get the most out of Twitter. This is going back a while, but it was really effective, and I managed to accumulate about 80 subscribers. I went on the following month to do the same for Facebook, then Linkedin. With each list I created, I segmented the subscribers into the different topic that they had signed up for.*

*I wasn't selling anything as this point, but I knew I would be further down the line. I continued creating content (blog posts mainly) around the topics and each time I published I had a list of people I could send the link to who I knew were interested.*

*I did this with each topic for a couple of months, then started to include a call to action offering free reviews of their Twitter, Facebook or Linkedin activity with suggestions on how they could improvement engagement. Once I'd done the review I would then offer a paid for managed social media service, and tah dah - my business was up and running.*

It worked because I understood their needs. I had made them aware through my emails just how effective social media could be for their business, and I had established know, like and trust. By talking to them about their challenges with Twitter, Facebook or Linkedin (in some cases all three) they knew I was on their wavelength and 'got it'. Only one of the emails was about a free review but I was adding value that wouldn't cost them anything.

Only one of the emails mentioned a paid for service, and by this point they knew me and my business well enough to know that I knew what I was talking about.

### Setting Goals

As with any marketing activity it's important to set goals and objectives from the outset, otherwise how will you know if it was a success?

Setting goals will help shape the content of your email and define what you will consider as a successful campaign.
Keep it simple at first;

- Define who you are sending your campaign to, which audience segment?

- Why are you sending them this email?

- What action do you want them to take?

- What are the benefits for the reader if they take this action?

Further down the line, once you've sent a few campaigns you can start to dig deeper and compare Click Through Rates and Open Rates, but we'll look at them in more detail a bit later on.


If you decide to send a monthly newsletter then commit to a day every month that the newsletter will go out. Consistency shows that you are reliable and will result in higher open rates. Always make sure you have something of interest and value to say, don't just send for the sake of it.

If you've segmented your audience but want to send them a general monthly newsletter as well, ask for their permission first. It might mean that some months they get more than one email from you - make this clear from the get go so they don't get overwhelmed and unsubscribe.

## Testing and Measuring

Some emails will get opened more than others, and that's just the way it is unfortunately. You're relying a lot on the mood of the recipient, how busy they are, what device they're reading it on, the time of day they receive it. But there are things you can do maximise the success of your campaign.

Every single area of an email can be tested and measured for effectiveness, but it does require you to be a little analytical. If you're new to email marketing, then I suggest trying this on an email that you send out consistently i.e. your monthly newsletter then once you see improvements in open rates and click throughs you can apply the changes to your nurturing sequence or email campaigns.

Some of the most commonly tested areas are;
- Subject lines
- Calls to action
- Button colours
- Fonts and text colours
- Date & time sent

Subject lines are where you can have the biggest impact. This is the first thing that the reader will see in their inbox so make it enticing enough for them to open it.

Try using questions, including their first name, posing a dilemma or the start of a story that continues in the body of the email, for example;

'Have you made this mistake <<first name>>?'
'Should I close my business?'
'My mum once told me <<first name>> that..'

If you can include the topic of the free opt-in that they originally sign up for then you'll see an increased open rate;

'Have you made this Facebook mistake <<first name>>?
'Is Facebook taking over my business?'
'My mum's on Facebook, what can I do..'

Try changing up the Call To Action too. Make sure you have tracking turned on so you can see which links have been clicked, and vary where you direct people to. Include links to your YouTube channel and encourage people to subscribe or invite them to join your Facebook Group or Page to deepen the connection.

Remember, keep it simple at first then when you're more confident you can build momentum and play around with different sections of the email to see what works.

## What to write

Are you one of those that just doesn't think they have anything of value or interest to say on a consistent monthly basis? You're not on your own - I hear this all the time.

The simple fact is that everyone is different. What I write in my emails won't apply to your audience, so I'm not a huge fan of those lists that say '100 things to write in an email' - know the ones I mean? They can be a starting point sure, but one thing I've learnt is that if you don't write with sincerity, in your own voice and align your message with your brand then your subscribers will see right through you.

Everything you write, from social media updates to sales copy, should be written in YOUR tone of voice. It's guaranteed to sound authentic and genuine.

How do you find your tone of voice? Simple, write as you speak. Now, I'm a Yorkshire girl but my copy isn't littered with Yorkshire slang (you'd never understand a word!) but I do have Yorkshire traits that come across in my writing. I tend to be direct, without the fluffy stuff and get straight to the point. This is very apparent in my videos and webinars, but it does make me relatable, and that's what makes the difference. If you try to imitate someone else, you will come across as false.

So, when you're thinking about what to say in your emails, have a think about recent conversations you've had about your industry - can you share your thoughts with your subscribers and ask for their opinions? The call to action could be to continue the discussion over on Linkedin or your Facebook page.
What's happening in your subscriber's world? Is there some time or money saving tool that you can review and recommend? Include a blog post and relevant links. Maybe even make a video and add the link.

Always, always make sure your email content is focused around your subscriber, what interests them and focus on how you can add value.

**Action Steps**
- How can you segment your list?
- What is your goal / aim / purpose of emailing?
- When will you send your regular email communication out?
- Start to track click through rates and open rates on your regular email communications so you can test and measure further down the road.
- Set up a system for collating topics / resources you can talk about or link to.

# Chapter Seven

# Email Nurturing

**In this chapter**
Email nurturing is the process of taking your new subscribers from being just a name on a list to your new best friend. A best friend who knows, likes and trusts you enough to hang out with you, and ultimately buy from you.

It's like a game of courtship, you wouldn't ask for their hand in marriage on the first date. You'd take your time getting to know them, what makes them tick, finding common ground and building a trusting relationship and it's just the same with email nurturing.

And as with all things Digital Marketing it takes time and there are one or two steps you need to follow to make your new friend feel welcome and loved.

Currently they are sitting at the top of your sales funnel, with very little awareness about you or your brand. However, they came to sign up to your list, they have trusted you with an important asset, their email address - don't blow it now by going all in with your sales message. In fact, very few of your emails should be about either you or the sales pitch.

Every time a subscriber sees your email in their inbox you want them to feel a sense of "Ah, hello old friend," and look forward to reading what you have to share as they know they will get value from it, learn something or at the very least be left with a sense of time well spent after reading your communication.

Think about it, you already know what their pain point is through whichever free download they signed up for. If you suddenly start talking to them about something completely unrelated, why should they stick around?

However, if you talk about their pain point and can offer valid solutions they'll be positively bursting to open your email. They know you'll make their life easier in some way, they'll value your input.

If you fill your email with 'Hey, look what I've been doing,' 'Aren't I great?' what incentive is that for them to stay subscribed?

People want to feel special, individual and important.

## Using Email Nurturing to Build Know, Like, Trust

So, what can you do to nurture your subscriber through your sales funnel whilst building know, like and trust as well developing a deeper more meaningful connection?

The first step is to create an email sequence that's all about the topic they just downloaded. Here's the sequence that I use;

**Monthly Newsletter - sent 1st Thursday in every month**
- 1st email (sent immediately on sign up) -Welcome and thank you, how can I help

- 2nd email (sent 2 days later) What to expect and how you can get involved

- 3rd email (sent 5 days later) Let's connect on social media

**Free opt-in (starts immediately on sign up)**
- 1st email - Free download and thank you

- 2nd email (2 days later) How are you getting on & top tips (around opt in)

- 3rd email (5 days later) Where to find more, need any help, join the Facebook group
- 4th email (10 days later) How did it help you? Offer free 1 to 1 call & website link for more info

These email sequences are fairly standard but to make them stand out and to get opened;

- I include the pain point in the subject line
- I add even more value by suggesting further tips
- I invite them to connect with me on other channels, primarily my Facebook Group
- I personalise the email using their first name where it would naturally fit
- I direct them to the website for more information

How often you should send an email will depend on your sales funnel process.

Send more frequently in the early days to build the connection then as time progresses reduce the frequency.

## Moving your prospects through the sales funnel

I've learnt the hard way that making the switch between teaching and selling in your email sequence can be;
- Uncomfortable
- Complicated
- Overwhelming
- Disappointing
- A LOT OF WORK

But I'm glad I've learnt because I can now share my experience with others and stop them from making the same mistakes.

Flicking the switch from providing value to selling a service can feel uncomfortable, particularly if you're new to selling online (i.e you're not an eCommerce store), and even more so if you've always followed the traditional business model of exchanging time for money.

Of course you still need to sell your services by nurturing your prospects through your sales funnel, but your approach will be different depending on the actual service.

And therein lies my point - not every sales funnel is the same, and not every email nurturing sequence is the same but they ALL follow the same process.
- Exchange email address for free download (top of funnel)
- Educate by adding even more value (top of funnel)
- Connect to build deeper connection (Middle of funnel)
- Offer / sales introduced (Bottom of funnel)

What content is in each email is entirely down to you, your target audience needs and your intended outcome.

The one email that EVERY funnel needs is the CONVERSION email. This is when you switch from providing free value to introducing your offer and inviting subscribers to take a course of action.

Conversion emails are all about switching from teaching to selling. They usually include a link to a webinar, a masterclass, a livestream or even a pre-recorded masterclass (you will have done it live first to make sure it works).

This where the 'magic' happens. Your webinar or masterclass will be 90% education, and 10% sales which will come right at the end.

Once your webinar ends (with a strong and immediate call to action) you will need to have a further nurturing sequence in place for those that didn't 'buy on the night'. These emails should be benefit driven, include testimonials from those that have bought and if you want to instil urgency you can include a countdown timer to when you will be closing the doors.

Putting energy and effort into creating the automated sequences and a live webinar is time consuming but oh my word, when those sales start to hit there really is no feeling like it.

Action Steps
- Map out your nurturing sequence
- Use the tips to encourage open rates
- Think about what your conversion email will direct people to; a webinar for example
- Plot your conversion email follow up sequence for once the webinar ends.

"If you are not putting in the time and energy to succeed, then someone else will and you have no right to complain when they take what was yours".

Paul Roetzer, PR2020

# Chapter Eight

# Your 28 Day Digital Road Map

We're almost at the end of our time together - well done, you made it through to the end.
Now it's time to put everything you have learnt into practice and to start building your email list.

The map is broken down into weekly and daily steps, and each activity should take less than an hour per day but of course you can spend more time on the task if you have it or feel the need.

Are you ready to begin? Feel free to buy a new notebook by the way! Don't forget to join the Facebook Group too – search Digital Marketing Made Easy.

**WEEK 1 - ON YOUR MARKS..**
**Day 1 - Inventory Day**

**Personal**
Where are you at right now? If you have a million business ideas floating around in your head write them down.

**Marketing**
Could your existing marketing be better? Where do you think it's lacking? If you feel something is working, what is it and why do think that is?
Get everything out of your head and down onto paper - it will help with clarity, focus and instil your commitment to do something about it (plus the added bonus of sleeping better!)

## Day 2 - Identify your target audience and ideal client
Getting crystal clear on who you can help is super important. Niche down as far as you can and be laser focused on who you can serve best.

## Day 3 - Create Your Survey
Let this run for a week minimum or for the rest of this challenge - there will opportunities to tweak elements of your map along the way so stay flexible depending on the results.

## Day 4 - Identify where your audience hangs out
Which social channels do they visit, which Facebook groups. Make a list so you can go back to them.

## Day 5 - Identify Pain Points
Using the list, you created on Day Four go back and look to see what they are talking about. What are their struggles and pain points? What do they need help with? Can you provide part of the solution through your content i.e. blog post, videos?

## Day 6 - Start Building Your Connections & Engaging
Again, using the list you created on Day Four, start connecting with people, commenting on their posts and building know, like and trust. This should be an ongoing part of your overall strategy so make sure you build time in every day to do this. It might even be on your phone whilst commuting or on an evening when watching TV - just make sure you do it regularly and often.

## Day 7 - Content Creation
We'll start creating the content later, for now just brainstorm ideas of blog posts, videos, social media posts that you can share with your audience that will add value. Remember to think of ways you can repurpose each piece of content to make sure it works hard for you.

## WEEK 2 - Build the momentum

### Day 8 - List Building
What can you give away for free that provides value, showcases you as the expert and will go 20% of the way to solving your prospects pain point? Write it down, create mind maps, go whiteboard crazy. When you have 2 or 3 really solid ideas ask your audience (regardless of how many you have) which appeals to them most. Consider the format but a simple 1 or 2-page PDF guide will be absolutely fine - don't use this as a reason to procrastinate or put it off - JUST DO IT!

### Day 9 - Create Your Free Download

### Day 10 - Create A Landing Page or Add to your website
For more detailed instructions on this you can view a tutorial here >>
https://www.herdingcatsdigital.com/bookresources

### Day 11,12,13 and 14
Write An Email Nurturing Sequence

For more detailed instructions on this you can view a tutorial here
https://www.herdingcatsdigital.com/bookresources

## WEEK 3 - READY, SET..

### Day 15 - Content Creation
Brainstorm the additional content you can create around your free download that you can share over social media.

### Day 16 - Content Collaboration
Is there anyone you can collaborate with that compliments your business? Can you tap into their audience and vice versa? This is a great way to open up new doors and new opportunities.

## Day 17 - Adding Analytics
Make sure you have Google Analytics in place as well as making a note of how many followers / fans you have before you start any activity. You can review it again once the campaign is over to see the results.

## Day 18, 19 20 & 21 - Batch Create Content
If you have videos to record, podcasts to record, blog posts to write I find it works well if you batch create everything. Also use this time to source any stock images you might need.

## WEEK 4 - GO!
## Day 22 - Review and Edit Content
Review, edit and proofread all your content including your email nurturing sequence, make sure all the links work and go to the right places. Ask for second opinions on your copy if you're not sure of anything but always go with your gut feeling.

## Day 23 - Plan ahead
If you're scheduling any content then allow a couple of days for sourcing images, finding appropriate hashtags and save them on Google Drive or Dropbox so you have instant access to them on any device (in case a super important scheduled post fails and you really need it to go out!).

## Day 24 - Check-in with Collaborators
If you're collaborating with anyone check you're all on the same page and know what each other is doing.

## Day 25 - Set targets / goals / ideal outcomes
By now you should be feeling super confident and inspired so set yourself some targets and goals. For example how many subscribers would you link to sign up over the next 30 days? Keep it realistic but don't be afraid to push for more!

## Day 26 - Reflect & Review

Take some deep breaths, some time out and review everything you've done so far. You've already achieved more than most entrepreneurs just by showing up every day and taking action.

## Day 27 - Share, share, share

Add that link everywhere and anywhere that you can. Talk about it in Facebook Groups, create conversations on Linkedin, deliver a livestream, add it to you email signature and most important of all - don't give up!

## Day 28 - CELEBRATE

Whoo hoo, you've done it! You're sign-ups are coming in, your email list is building and believe it or not people will already be talking about you. WELL DONE, YOU'RE AWESOME.


Ready to find out more? I mentioned at the start of our journey together that launching a membership site was one of my ultimate goals, and I'm delighted to say that I am well on my way!

Would you like to be one of the first to join? Head over to www.herdingcatsdigital.com/memberswaitlist to find out all the details.

# Final Words

It's all about you

It would be unfair of me to finish this book and not talk about you, after all you are the most important asset in your business.

It doesn't matter if you're a millionaire or a fledgling entrepreneur, if you don't have the right mindset to start out with then your journey will be much tougher.

Now, let me state that I am not trained in NLP or any kind of psychology but after building successful businesses and equally failing I've learnt that if your head isn't in the right place then not just business but life in general can be hard going.

Building a business online takes hard work, consistency and patience not to mention effort and showing up every single day in one form or another.

Even when your business gets off the ground you still have to keep a clear, focused head and a positive mindset.
For some people that might come naturally, for me it doesn't. I have to work to on it every day and occasionally take time away from everything until the cloud and confusion lift.
You can get tons of advice and help online but honestly, you need to find what works for you. If you're a morning person then develop a morning routine that sets that you up for the day. It could be meditation, positive affirmations, visualisation or reading from a motivational book. Equally if you're a night owl, honour that and create a routine that works for you.

Keep a journal - even if you only write in it once a month. It's a handy reminder of where you've been and how far you've come. When you're having a bad day or you're struggling to make sense of it all and wondering why the hell you got into this in first place take a flick back through the pages and remind yourself why you started out in the first place.

Surround yourself with like-minded, positive people who understand the journey you're on. You may find that you lose a couple of friends along the way and that's OK, maybe they weren't supposed to be part of your plan.

Above all else, celebrate the joy of being you. You are unique, you are here for a reason and life is too damn short not to make the most out of it. Take risks once in a while and follow your own path.

# Acknowledgements

I never thought I'd get this far in writing a book to be honest, and I definitely wouldn't have done if it hadn't been for the support of my amazing husband Mark who has been my editor, chief champion and nagging voice of 'have you written that book yet?' Thank you, my love.

Massive thanks to Holly, for painstakingly reading every draft I created and listening to me talk about this book endlessly, and to Mary for sense checking the words, and action steps!

To Daniel, my son for believing in me always and being my absolute rock.

Thank you to my online community for all the love and support as we continue on this wild and crazy journey together.

# About the author

Catherine Skeet-Yaffe is the founder of Herding Cats Digital, Digital Marketing Made Easy. Cat set up the business with a mission to empower, educate and support entrepreneurs to grow their online authority and presence so that they can effortlessly build a successful business whilst living their ideal life – something she strives to do every single day.

Cat has been featured on local radio and in various magazines including Cosmopolitan, Red and online platforms such as Huffington Post, Medium and Thrive Global sharing her knowledge of Digital Marketing.

When not working Cat spends time with her family and friends and beloved cats Jenson and Button (she's also a fan of F1!).

You can find out more about Cat here.
Website: www.herdingcatsdigital.com
Instagram: @digitalmarketingmadeeasy
Twitter: @herdingcatsdigi
Linkedin: CatherineYaffe
Youtube: Digital Marketing Made Easy
iTunes Podcast: Digital Marketing Made Easy

CPSIA information can be obtained
at www.ICGtesting.com
Printed in the USA
BVHW032308221222
654901BV00005B/27